PeeWee, I Swear I'm not Lying!

Experience Changes Lives…Or So I Think!

Anthony Norton

Dedication

"All I'm trying to do is survive and make good out of the dirty, nasty, unbelievable lifestyle that they gave me"
-Tupac Shakur

This book is dedicated to the reader of the quote above. I once were you and still am. Also, I want to dedicate this book to Ms. Blue (who's probably married now), my middle school reading teacher. Thanks for making me read out loud when you knew my reading level was on a fourth-grade level, I am forever thankful!

Acknowledgment

First and foremost, I want to express my gratitude towards God. If it wasn't for Him, I would have given up on this book a long time before I finished it. God never allowed me to put down my pen, which is why you all have this book in your hands.

Secondly, I want to thank every reader that took the time out to read my book. I am crying out of sheer gratitude right now as my devotion for this project will finally meet its end result. The fact that people are reading my book is an immense blessing, and it means a lot to me. Thank you for your undying love and support.

About the Author

Anthony Norton has spent his childhood curating different stories while sitting at his kitchen counter. Among his hobbies was to pretend that Opera was interviewing him, even though he was not a great reader back in middle school.

Anthony Norton devoted a major chunk of his energy to completing this book as nothing brings him more pleasure than when people read and enjoy his work. His book is about the importance of perspective, and how experiences can shape and change human lives.

Preface

This book offers a glimpse into the significance of human perspective. Among the many lessons it holds is one that highlights the role of experiences, and the path one selects for himself. Furthermore, it teaches one that he must correct his perspective in order to move in the right direction.

Secondly, this book lays emphasizes on the teachings of the church and reflects how God guides us towards the right path.

Last, but not the least, the book touches upon the importance of good company. Good companions guide you towards the light, while bad companions push you far into the depths of darkness. Your life is a sum of your experiences, and your experiences are brought by the company you keep. So, make sure it is worth keeping.

Contents

Page Blank Left Intentionally

Chapter 1- Welcome Home Fool!

"I wonder if heaven got a ghetto?"

-Tupac Shakur

Today marks the beginning of the last week of summer. Usually, this time around, I feel quite gathered up and composed, since school begins in only a week. But not this summer, as my friend, my boy, PeeWee, is coming home, finally! See, my boy PeeWee, whose real name is Willie, has been gone since the last day of school. Every summer, he has to go visit his rusty ass daddy for custody reasons (quoted words from Ms. Joe-Ann).

However, this summer was a little different from any other summer. Usually, everyone would be less active, posted inside, or under Ms. Sandy's cornerstore tree, due to the hell blazing weather. However, this summer, while PeeWee was in Maryland enjoying the mountains and block parties, I was stuck here in Muck City taking on the fiery summer, quite literally.

To be real, I am not sure if Maryland even has mountains. I just want to make sure that it looks like PeeWee had a much better summer than I did! The mountains seem like a great comparison to the scorching heat that I had to endure. Honestly, the visits to his daddy every summer weren't exactly fun for PeeWee either, but he at least got to leave the city for a while. He got to travel and experience different things every summer. I have never had that opportunity in my life.

Raised in a house on section 8 made things difficult for mama. It was hard for her to meet our expenses, so asking for a summer vacation outside Belle Glade was like asking for a trip outside the state of Florida. However, having a best friend like PeeWee made things preferable. Just being able to march down the street to his crib, playing videogames with him, and getting away from my reality kept my sixteen-year-old mind at peace.

PeeWee's mother lives in section 8 as well. Their financial situation is similar to that of ours. However, his mother gets a check for the treatment of his baby brother, Jaylen, every month for his disability. Due to this money, they have a little bit of room to stretch out their expenses and live comfortably.

It even allows them to eat an extra bowl of cereal in the morning or five pieces of chicken instead of four for dinner. This was one of my favorite reasons for sleeping over at his place on Friday nights. Willie has one of the most entertaining houses on the block due to the many personalities inside it. Now, when I say 'many' personalities, I mean, astonishingly bizarre and yet quite loveable people. Then again, that's what I feel. Perhaps you may not share my opinion.

On Saturday mornings, I usually watch his older sister and her friends twerk to 90's Uncle Luke, while his two older brothers stay down in the basement, counting drug money and bagging grains of cocaine. Alright, so they 'earn' a lot more than just disability money on the side. That's one other reason I like them so much. They are my favorite people because they know how to live life. They get everything they want with ease.

While on one hand that is true, on another, there is always the threat of the Police Department looming over their heads. The police could bust down their door any day of the week. They are just as under suspicion of the Police as Ms. Sandy's store for a drug bust. Although PeeWee's house is the spot, I would never get too comfortable there because I am aware of the things that happen over there. At any moment, I know the police could kick in the door but that never keeps me from going to play videogames, or watching PeeWee's sister twerk around. May be that's how it is in life. We only recognize the danger of fire when we get burned. I feel the same way. There isn't any harm in visiting my best friend until something goes wrong at his place.

So, like every summer when PeeWee returns, I go to his place and I did the same this time. As I stand outside in the windy air, I almost feel an uncontrollable urge to turn away and leave. However, I just can't get the videogames waiting for me out of my head. So, I push the uneasiness and knock on the door of PeeWee's crib.

PeeWee's Crib......

[Knock, Knock]

"Who is it?" I hear a grim voice from the inside. I know this voice all too well. I hear it regularly.

"It's me, Ms. Joe-Ann. Is Willie home?" I ask innocently, hoping against hope that PeeWee's mother wouldn't find anything sinister in my voice.

"Who is a damn me?" I hear another grim reply from inside but like always, I shrug it off. She has always been a little rough around the edges when she's drunk. She opens the door with the smell of natural ice on her breath.

"Why didn't you say it was you out there, you big ass head? I thought it was Mr. Johnson looking for rent! Now, that you are here, go on ahead, PeeWee's in his room, wide awake. You know he doesn't sleep at noon!" Ms. Joe-Ann nearly yells at me while I tumble over Jaylen's toys.

"Man, wake your ass up, your mama is in the kitchen, going off about this nasty room. I don't see anything changed much about you, nappy head." I say all this very fast as I walk into PeeWee's room and see him lying sprawled on his bed with his room all scattered with his things.

I can't control my excitement at his sight. I need to know more about his trip to his father's place.

PeeWee wakes up as I shake him a little harder. *"What's good, brother?"* He asks me the second he made sense of where he was. *"I miss you man, you don't understand how delighted I am to be back in Florida."* He adds, nearly beaming at me.

"First off nigga, welcome home. But delighted? When did you put the word "delighted" into your vocabulary? You spend a week longer than usual in Maryland, now you come home with an entirely new vocabulary? I tell you what, T.J Henderson, meet me outside on the porch, Mr. Delighted!" I say to him chuckling as I exit the room.

Getting your best friend back for even one week of the summer holidays is worth it! I can say that because I got my PeeWee back!

Chapter 2- Keisha's Son P.J

"For every dark night, there's a brighter day"

-Tupac Shakur

"Damn bro, it takes that long to come outside? And why didn't you bring me some of your mama's homemade sugarcane juice? You know she would want me to have it anyway."

I ask PeeWee shrewdly as he walks out on the porch empty-handed. One of the perks of visiting him includes great food and additional things that I can eat over at his place. Nonetheless, seeing him come out without my favorite juice feels quite disappointing.

"Man whatever you know, Mom's wanted me to clean my room and pick up my little brother's toys and shit," PeeWee said, sounding jovial to be home. He looks at me like I am wasting his time or something. I feel a bit taken aback by that. Generally, PeeWee enjoys having me around just as much as I enjoy being at his place. However, it doesn't seem like that today.

"What's up though? You hasten me out the house like you got something important to tell me." He asks me to know why exactly I am there.

I inhale deeply to keep my nerves calm. I can't quite figure out what's wrong with my boy PeeWee. *"There you go with that bullshit again!"* I exclaim as he starts laughing.

"You hasten me out the house like you got something important to tell me," I repeat in my squeaky PeeWee voice.

I carry on. *"Cut the shit out, peanut brain, a lot has changed since you left big homie,"* I inform PeeWee.

As I say that, I realize, I can't really explain anything to my boy. I always get a little hesitant on particular subjects. Even now I wasn't sure if I wanted to tell PeeWee, or act as if I had no knowledge of everything that went down here over the summer.

PeeWee can sometimes have a running faucet as a mouth, but at this point, I am the one with the loose lips, I take a deep breath before opening my mouth to flush out all the information I have.

"Grab a chair, homie." I take another deep breath,

hoping that my words do not come back to haunt me.

"So... First off, you know how lazy niggas be during the summer." I try to get started with the conversation.

"Yeah." PeeWee replies with a curious face.

"Well, I wish I could say the same for this one. To be honest, the city is quite messed up."

"Do you remember lil P.J.?" PeeWee is looking even more confused as I continue, *"You don't remember Lil P.J.? Big ears, dirty feet, Keisha's son, PAP JUNIOR!"*

"Okay, YEAH! I remember him." PeeWee sounds all excited as he recognizes the person I was referring to.

"What's this badass been up to?" I hang my head low, with teardrops accumulating in my eyes.

"He's dead, and elder Mr. Davidson killed him," I replied.

"Damn! Mr. Davidson? How did that happen? I thought he was saved or whatever?" PeeWee says with a look on his golden biscuit face that shows he is shaken.

"Hold up bro. Let me go check on the sausages. I got them boiling in the kitchen..."

Five minutes later...

He returned from the kitchen and then I ask him again, *"You still haven't brought me some of your mama's homemade special sugar cane juice!"*

"Bro, we don't have any, otherwise you would have been sipping some of it right now! So...Tell me...What happened?" PeeWee sounds eager to know as he sits on the edge of his seat.

"Honestly bro," I mutter slowly, feeling a bit salty about the juice situation. *"I heard that one Thursday night, Mr. Davidson didn't go to bible study... They say he was feeling a little under the weather. Now, the same night, lil P.J. claimed to steal Mr. Davidson's grandson's dirt bike, the crazy one that throws fire out the exhaust pipes. Word on the streets is that Pookie from 100th & Ave paid him to get the bike.*

Around 10 O'clock that night, they say Mr. Davidson was sitting at his kitchen table reading his bible, when suddenly he heard his wooden side gate closed shut. Elder Davidson instantly peeked from his sliding glass door, and watched this black figure rumble over materials in his tool shed.

Honestly bro, I think the old man was done with watching his things walk away daily. Plus, he had just buried his wife a month ago. How stressful is that? So I kind of understand where he was coming from. Anyway, so after seeing the black shadow, Mr. Davidson fired off a shot, catching P.J in the hip, so it had obviously become very difficult for him to escape. Some say, the first shot was a headshot, but that never happened. The neighbor next door to Mr. Davidson saw it all happening. Now, he said, the first shot was a hip shot, sending P.J. to the ground. P.J then tried doggy hustling towards the side gate, while blood soaked his jeans, then caught another shot in the kidney, which caused him to collapse just inches away from the wooden gate.

The crazy thing is that Mr. Davidson had threatened P.J. a few weeks prior to the day he got killed. Mr. James looked lil P.J in his eyes and said: "Son, if you don't change your disrespectful ways and keep acting as everyone owes you something, you won't live to see fifteen. I tell you, son, nobody owes you a damn thing." P.J stepped an inch closer to Mr. James' face, looked him square in the eyes and told him: "A drunk like you can't tell me nothing. You lost everything you ever owned... I see why that old bitch left you. Fuck outta here shit turd."

It takes PeeWee over thirty seconds to utter a word and all he says is *"Damn!!"*

I give PeeWee a few seconds, but when I realize he has nothing to say, I continue.

"Brother." I begin speaking with a very soft and humble voice. *"If you would've seen the video from Mr. Davidson's neighbor surveillance camera, you would've felt the agony, he was only fourteen, bro. But at the same time, you gotta understand Mr. Davidson's situation. He's 68. Lives alone. I mean... that sucks! Anybody living that way would be paranoid."*

"Yeah, I could only imagine," PeeWee says appearing very depressed.

I am not yet done with my story so I carry on, *"Not only that PeeWee, the police came to the scene and didn't even try to save him. They just watched him drown in his own blood. When Keisha arrived to identify the body, she fell to her knees, let out a loud cry, and demanded Mr. Davidson to be arrested. Well, he couldn't be charged with anything, as according to the law, P.J. was trespassing.*

While Keisha cried tears of blood, the neighbors didn't even bother to give her a freaking shoulder to cry on.

It was a dreadful night. I went straight home, and prayed to God. I prayed for hours, and I didn't really understand why, because I was basically repeating the same shit. (God please mend Keisha's broken heart.) My heart weighted so heavily for both families. Keisha losing her youngest son, and the church turning their back on Mr. Davidson. Those Catholic, God-fearing Christians should be ashamed of themselves. A tragic moment in the community, but a tragedy that was bound to happen."

I take a deep breath and stare down at the porch. I notice from the side of my eye that Willie was petrified. A little part of me felt that PeeWee was overcoming Willie, and at any moment, he was to vomit something ignorant or disrespectful out of his mouth.

So, before he could say a word that could jeopardize our fourteen-year friendship, I tried starting up another conversation. PeeWee knows me well, and before I try to divert a conversation, he changes the subject himself.

ANTHONY NORTON

Chapter 3- Fat Sam's Pizza Shop

"I'd rather die like a man, than live like a coward"

- Tupac Shakur

"How's your mom, bro? I haven't seen her since the week I left for Maryland." PeeWee inquired.

"Mom's doing fine. She a little upset with me right now." I state, with my tone making it sound like I had let down my mother.

"Ant!" PeeWee kissed his teeth like he was bothered. I wasn't sure what he had to say, but I could feel it was something he was unsettled about. He turned his lips upwards and cocked them to the side as if he just had a stroke. Before I could say anything, PeeWee proceeded.

"You know how Ms. Tina could be... the devil this, the devil that. Did she ever think maybe the church she goes to has the devil inside it? I mean, she puts so much trust into a white Jesus."

"First off Jesus is not white, he's black!" I interrupt and make my point with full confidence, but I could tell PeeWee didn't know much about Jesus, nor my mother. Having a Christian mother raise you like a Jehovah witness can really fuck you up psychologically. Some years we celebrate my birthday, some years we don't even acknowledge it as a day I was born on, and my age just increases by one in number. So for two years straight, I believe since I was eight, my birthday had never come. However, that defeats the purpose of mom being right for once in a lifetime, and I couldn't let PeeWee think otherwise.

"I know sometimes mom-dukes can be a little too Godly, but she has a real valid reason for beating me with her vegetable oil." In black homes, we refer to vegetable oil as blessing oil. Being raised in the south, vegetable oil is our substitute for holy water. Parents use it to *"remove the demons,"* but I doubt it does anything.

"What happened?" PeeWee pulled back his dreads with a laughable look on his face. *"It's getting hot out here,"* I said, trying to change the subject, but Whoopie golden locks weren't falling for it.

"Naw bro, you did something stupid. Don't try changing the subject." PeeWee is very eager to know what I had done. He even offers to get me some sugarcane juice.

"Well let me see," I answer, dragging all of my words, and muttering softly. Hoping that some words would slip by unnoticed.

I cleared my throat. (Coughing)

"Well, you know how I got that job at Sam's pizza shop before school ended right? Well, I ended up getting a little too comfortable and got fired," PeeWee began laughing like I knew he would.

"But listen to me, bro." I try to strengthen my case, *"Everything was going fine. I was due for an upcoming raise, and Sam was getting ready to move me from delivery driver to manager, until I did the most idiotic thing one could ever do.*

While delivering, I had Tay charcoal black ass in the car with me. Before you speak on the situation, allow me to explain what happened.

So, this is how it went. I was riding down Avenue J after

delivering to Monica's house. That's when my gas light came on, so I headed towards Ms. Sandy's store for gas. A quarter mile from the store, I saw Tay standing up near the stop sign. He waved me down to stop, so I did." He said: "Ant, you going to the loading ramp party this weekend?"

I don't know Tay, and why you always smelling like a damn carpet burn? I literally had to hold my nose to protect my lungs from being polluted. Somehow my conversation with Tay led him inside my car.

Tay was always good with slipping and sliding through conversations for his own gain. (Stank ass mudfish.)

Tay being in the car wasn't the part that got me fired. What really got me fired was an incident that occurred during my second delivery, when the customer called the store and made a complaint to Fat Sam about their pizza smelling like weed, and being eaten from. Tay was smoking in my mom's car and had taken a slice of pizza from the box while I was in the store paying for gas.

Sam called me the next morning about it and requested that I turn in my uniforms. I confronted Tay about it, he tells me 'He never tried a plain cheese pizza before.'"

PeeWee fell backward out of his chair laughing.

"So how did your mom find out about it?" PeeWee asks.

I knew he wasn't going to stop laughing but I still answered his question, *"Fat Sam and mom go to the same Church, so Sam told her everything. The real issue mom had was me being around Tay, and knowing about his heavy drug addiction, and knowing about his several visits to rehab, and you know knowing that he did not want to change."*

"Man you know better than to trust Tay's stank ass." PeeWee says holding his breath to speak and resumes laughing hard.

Watching PeeWee laugh sent me into a daydream, and I realized or rather admitted the stupidity of my actions. With Tay's use of cocaine and him being so rebellious, I don't know what I was thinking. Tay was my friend, a friend that had lost both his parents at a young age. Imagine being ten-years-old and seeing your father being killed by the Gang Lords. Imagine your mother being raped and murdered right in front of your eyes all because of an *"I owe you."*

My mother does not understand my friendship with Tay. I wonder if anybody does. Mom was extremely angry and she drowned me in blessing oil for weeks. Yelling at me, *"Tay is not your type of energy, you lost your job being around him. If you don't start staying away from him, the next thing you lose can be your life."*

"Mama is never happy when I do something stupid," I say in an attempt for some face-saving while glancing over the road.

"PeeWee there goes Mr. Johnson heading this way. Better let your mom know." I draw his attention to the white man approaching his house.

PeeWee opens the door and yells inside. *"Mom?"*

"What, boy?" His mom yells back.

"There goes Mr. Johnson on the sidewalk heading this way."

"Shit! Tell him I got no damn money, he going to have to come back on the first." Ms. Joe-Ann shouts back to reply.

PeeWee shut the door close with a distraught look,

knowing he had to come up with a lie quick because Mr. Johnson was getting near.

"How you doing fellas?" Mr. Johnson asks.

"Hi, Mr. Johnson." PeeWee and I both respond.

"Willie my son, your mother home?"

"No, Mr. Johnson she's not home. She went to the store she said she'll be back within an hour," PeeWee answers hoping his face does not make it evident that he's lying.

"Okay son, just make sure you let her know Mr. Johnson came by for the rent." Mr. Johnson demanded.

"Yes sir I will," PeeWee says attempting to create grounds for Mr. Johnson's early departure.

Mr. Johnson may be white but sure wasn't fooled by PeeWee's lies. He knew Ms. Joe-Ann was inside but he pretended to believe PeeWee and walked away. Mr. Johnson's unannounced stops really annoyed PeeWee. I could clearly see the annoyance as we sat in silence until Mr. Johnson was out of sight.

Nobody in the neighborhood liked being past the due date in paying rent. Mainly because Mr. Johnson would speak so loud and threaten to put the person, who would fail to clear his payments, out of his property. Everyone in the neighborhood knew Mr. Johnson as a nasty, white old devil who owned most of the property on our block, so even if the whole community wanted him gone, there is nothing they could have done about it. To be honest, I don't think the community wanted Mr. Johnson out as much as they talked about it, because his rent was very reasonable.

The jobs were limited, and the incomes were insufficient, which made it hard to pay the bills. Also, Mr. Johnson was always on the back of the person, who even paid a dollar short in rent. That was enough to drive anyone deranged, is it not?

Chapter 4- Mo'Nique

"Hate to sound sleazy, but tease me, I don't want it if it's that easy"

-Tupac Shakur

After PeeWee blew off some steam, I decided to tell him about my relationship with Mo'Nique. I was not sure if it was the right time to tell him about it. He did not like Mo'Nique much, which is why telling him about us had become a bit challenging. Many times, PeeWee suggested me to stay away from Mo'Nique. Mainly because of the rumors, but I mostly let them in from one ear and out the other.

Mo'Nique was a different kind of woman. I would literally have goosebumps in her presence. When I would be with her, everything would seem perfect. She had become very important to me, and explaining that to PeeWee is never going to be easy. Mo'Nique was beautiful. She wore this pink, bubble gum lip gloss that reflected off her beautiful dark skin, and my favorite jeans shorts exposed her muscular erotic thighs.

She had a very soft, soulful voice, and when she spoke, it would sound like Kurt Franklin's musical choir. Of course, Mo'Nique and I have a lot of sex. We have it as often as stray dogs do. However, it's not the physical intimacy that gets us closer, but rather, our conversations are where we connect the most. We talk a lot about her dark childhood, and the death of my father - things that many teens face in our community.

My biggest concern now is how PeeWee will react when I tell him that Mo'Nique and I were dating. For him, she is a whore that has slept with everybody in our neighborhood. Big Mac, who chilled up the block from where we lived, would tell us stories about how Mo'Nique would have sex with two to three guys a day - sometimes all at once. PeeWee believed what Big Mac said, but I never bought whatever Big Mac told.

Apparently, the more Big Mac lied, the fatter he got, but that's none of my business. Fortunately, my experience with Mo'Nique wasn't anything like Big Mac had told us. I'm glad I never believed any of his nonsense. I got my opportunity to witness it first hand, while forced to do community hours at Ms. Patterson's daycare. Anytime I got in trouble with mama, or she heard about any trouble caused by me, she would make me do community service hours as punishment. I don't know what good the hours of service were for, as it never did anything for me. When I found out that Mo'Nique did summer work at Ms. Patterson's daycare, I didn't mind picking up plastic and beer cans around the center. She turned out to be my motivation to work enthusiastically there.

Hell, if Ms. Patterson wanted me there for more than three hours a day, I could have done an entire shift unpaid. I made the most of every chance I had to let Mo'Nique know that I was interested in her. Though it was all for the wrong intentions. Sex was all I saw in Mo'Nique. It was the main reason I wanted to get with her. She wasn't fooled by my charm and only waited for the right time to speak about it.

One day, while picking up plastics from the playground area, Mo'Nique asked me, *"Anthony are you happy? What makes you happy?"* I wasn't ready for these questions. Maybe because my mind was dominated by lust. I was looking forward to *"Where you wanna do this? And how you wanna do it?"* That sure wasn't the case. However, before I could answer, Mo'Nique asked me the same question again, *"Anthony did you hear me? What makes you happy?"*

I replied, *"Girl I don't know. I guess being here with you."* It was not the best thing to say, but as far as I cared, I was just trying to figure out if she was really sexually healing, like the Marvin Gaye record.

Mo'Nique just stared at me with a look of disappointment and complained, *"You guess?!! Nigga! You ain't no different than the rest. A fast pass to some ass is all y'all care about. Where is the passionate care for me? I been raped and touched on by everyone in my step daddy family and my momma ears are plugged to everything I say."*

After exhaling out her disappointment and anger, she dropped her head into her lap. In a shivering voice, she continued, *"Anthony, when I was younger, just a little girl, my mother would tell me how much she hated me and accused me of trying to take on the role of being my step daddy's lover. I could never have imagined that my own mother would turn her back on me for a man.*

I cried out on many occasions, telling her how I was being sexually abused. She would say things like, "Tommy just showing you the way a guy supposed to touch and hold you." But it never felt right in my heart. There were times she would sit up in her bedroom late night drinking glasses of hard liquor. She would hear Tommy creeping into my bedroom and wouldn't do a thing. Who doesn't even rescue their own daughter?!" Heavy tears ran down Mo'Nique's cheeks into her cleavage. It drew my attention and I got distracted. Mo'Nique continued speaking, *"After he would get done, I would curl up and cry out a prayer, but they were never answered. So I don't ever look to the sky for no white Jewish man on a horse to save me. Therefore, I constantly seek for love. I desperately need an ounce of love I can get. Don't matter if it was through sex or just lounging around. I search for it in everything."*

"Damn." is all I could say. While still being a nigga, I couldn't help but fancy my chances of having sex with her. I wasn't sure about the Jewish man, but black Jesus spoke clearly to me. The same one that got me to stop thinking *"sex"* and motivated me to get to know her. I took one day at a time learning Mo-Mo (Mo'Nique). I also thought it was important to teach Mo-Mo about the black Jesus and so I did.

I wasn't ready to share my personal relationship with Mo-Mo to PeeWee and I doubt he would understand. As far as he knew, Mo'Nique slept with the entire neighborhood, and as far as I know, PeeWee never had a real relationship besides Janay dirty ass. So I didn't bother sharing mine with him.

Chapter 5- Sweet Maryland

"Behind every sweet smile, there is a bitter sadness that no one can see and feel"

-Tupac Shakur

"How was Maryland?" I asked PeeWee, scared that he caught me staring into space, which I doubt he did, as he's not the brightest street light standing. Street light standing was a term used by my mom. I don't really know what it means. I think it meant having good insights, or a nice overview. Sometimes, the truth is best left unsaid. PeeWee can wait to know about Mo'Nique. He must have a lot to speak about Maryland anyway.

"Maryland was sweet, bro." PeeWee replies. *"I attended many Go-Go's, and really got out to visit the city. Even Wale was back home showing the city love. You do know Wale, right?"* PeeWee asks. *"Yeah man, I know Wale. I been listening to him since his Attention Deficit album."* I answer with confidence, knowing he's one of the best rappers in the industry. *"I wasn't for sure bro, I just had to ask,"* PeeWee adds.

"What is a Go-Go?" I ask.

"A Go-Go is a style of partying in the tri-area of Maryland, D.C, and a small part of Virginia." However, PeeWee wasn't sure about attending many Go-Go's. I could tell how he was fumbling over his words. I have known PeeWee for quite some time, and I can tell when he's being honest, and when he isn't. I shake my head in a way as if I can picture the dance culture of Maryland. Honestly, my expressions are completely the opposite of my understanding. I have no idea of the kind of parties he is speaking about, in fact, I am not even putting in any effort to picture or imagine that culture.

"This summer, Maryland didn't let me down, or should I say my father finally let me out the house to experience what Maryland is really like. Despite the night, I arrived in Maryland, the police had my father's entire street blocked off. Nosy ass Ms. Jackie that lives next door said a policewoman was just shot while sitting in her patrol car. The same one that was giving my father a hard time last summer. Pops did say her day was coming too."

I look at PeeWee like he has lost his mind. *"Pete said that?"* I ask. *"Man your dad tripping."*

PeeWee didn't see anything wrong with his father's statement. Law poorly handled the community and he sure had his reasons to believe that his father had a point. When you live in a community that has a poor law and order situation, you tend to blame the law enforcing agencies for everything wrong that takes place there. It isn't completely wrong though. So I do not bother to say anything else, and allow him to carry on. I do feel his attitude reflected some sort of revenge or injustice he or his father had faced, but it is too early to draw any conclusions.

"Man, you remember my half-brother? He had just started working at Walmart a week before I got there, so my pops bought him a car. A little slider, something to get back and forth to work. Man, when I tell you we had that Lincoln all over south Maryland, imagine how crazy Maryland would have been! Me and my brother spent the entire summer hanging out with boujee inner-city girls. I'm talking 90's trick daddy thick chicks. You know the ones that wear the same jeans shorts daily just to show off their ass. And boy they've got an ass worth showing."

PeeWee is talking so fast that he stutters with a mouth full of slobber. *"Man!!! I had a blast, I met this chick by the name of Yasmin, Puerto Rican, and black. Most beautiful female I met."*

She better be worth a head turn to get this nigga stuttering and carrying on, I think to myself. Besides, I am so focused on Mo'Nique, my dark chocolate, that I am not interested in hearing about some light skinned, corn on the cob looking chick. PeeWee could see the look on my face, and stopped talking about her. He is not really going to talk to me about his emotions for her, in fact all he will speak about is her body, so we better speak of something that interests us both.

"Words can't explain how much fun I had in Maryland. Yeah, it was hot, but I really enjoyed this summer more than the previous ones." Our conversation continues, *"Why is that?"* I ask, resting my head into my hand. I have known PeeWee for so long that I knew something was up. I just couldn't put a hand on why he wanted me to side with him before he said what Maryland was really all about.

"I know you may not understand, but I will say anyway. I'm Gang related, I joined the black flags. Nothing like

brotherhood, fellowship, and attention from a couple of birds (females)."

"*NIGGA!*" Is all I could say, frustrated. Feeling very disappointed and stupid. At one point in life, PeeWee was someone I looked up to. Now, I am just not on this dummy's energy. "*First off, my nigga, stop your bullshit. Maybe your father letting you run wild in the city of Maryland was a monster mistake. Gang-related? Really? You one of the stupidest niggas I know. And your lust for attention, fellowship, and brotherhood, lets me know how weak-minded you really are. I'm your brother, and I wouldn't dare lead you into trouble, not even in times like those when we stole from Ms. Sandy's store. If you want fellowship, Pastor Jones church is open seven days a week, nearly 24 hours a day, so head down there and get your ass doing something there!*"

At this point, I could feel our friendship fading to black. "*Brotherhood?*" I ask again. "*Man, you don't see the lifestyle your brothers living? It won't be long before they get caught or end up on a garden road in the cemetery. You have some nerves to talk about attention! My mother is a single parent, never home, and serves the church more than she cares for my sister and I. Who's giving us attention?*

Bro! All I'm trying to say is that we should want more than what we are offered. Yeah, I love the hood and the homies too, but making it my day-to-day lifestyle until death, is something I am not interested in. These streets don't care for anybody - not even an innocent bystander!"

Chapter 6- Loading Ramp

"I wanna go in peace when I gotta die. On these cold streets, ain't no love, no mercy, and no friends"

-Tupac Shakur

"Just the other night at the block party, Tech 9's were firing off like fireworks at the loading ramp. A nigga was scared for his life bro, tripping and tumbling over women in short skirts, and dodging behind Chevy's and Toyota's, trying to protect my melon (head). Mama always said, 'call on the lord in time of trouble,' so I did. I closed my eyes, and started praying."

"Lord please have mercy on me, allow me to make it out of this hell war.

Forgive me for being blunt, but I only came to the block party to chill, and to show my rap game to these bitches.

Please don't go deaf ear to my fear, pour your blood on me, and make me invisible."

Sometimes, I find it funny how we forget about Jesus in times when we are happy and satisfied. As soon as we are struck by chaos and unrest, the first thing we automatically do is make a prayer. However, we can't keep waiting for an unfortunate event to happen in order to pray. I think about Jesus in good times too, but most of us remember Jesus only in times of trouble.

"Mama always said, 'when you pray, just talk to the lord as if he was one of your friends, as there is no certain way to pray,' so I took that into consideration. A certain way to pray was my least concern; I was caught in a restricted crossing zone. As I laid underneath a heated engine, I watched the bodies collapse helplessly. What could cause these circus animals to perform like this?" I asked myself. While innocent souls were taken, I closed my eyes for the second time, and began to pray once more."

"Lord please don't send any of these shots my way,

I'm not ready to leave this earth.

Mama still got past due bills, and I know she can't pay them herself.

Forgive me lord for the curse I have poured upon myself."

"We all find Jesus when trouble starts closing in. Agree?" PeeWee just nods his head agreeing with me, but I

can feel that he isn't totally agreeing. I feel that he thinks I am trying to make a case for his decision in Maryland to gangbang. PeeWee has this habit of focusing on the argument so much that at times he even misses the point of it. I do not want to continue any further with the discussion of his gang life in Maryland. There is no point of speaking about it if all his focus lies in winning the argument. I so wanted him to understand that I cared about him, and he needed to get his shit together.

"While I breathed carefully and tried not to be seen, I witnessed a little girl get shot and killed while sitting in the backseat of her mother's car. She was barely three, and I didn't understand why this crazy woman risked her child's life in these streets. Maybe she just wanted to hang out, lean up against cars, and drink 40's like it were the 90's.

The police arrived after the gun smoke cleared like always. Everyone stood over, and stared at the six bodies that laid lifeless, including that of the little girl, who was dragged out of the car by her mother.

My eyes were filled with blood, and my vision got blurry. I have seen too much within a short period of time, and my mind couldn't wrap around it."

I take a pause. It is not easy to talk about the incident, let alone being present in that situation. PeeWee appears to be thinking about something. Maybe he is trying to relate to this story. Again, I have to make sure he doesn't feel that I am trying to convince him that he will end up in a mess if he does not change the path he has chosen. Although I really want to give him some decent Jesus talk, right now, I am just sharing my experience with him without any purpose or motive.

"Bro, God spared me, that's a big fact. I could've easily been one of those six lifeless souls. I am so grateful. However, it's depressing that victims were used for God to get my attention.

As a kid, mama taught me to never question God's work, and to never doubt His ability."

PeeWee's mother calls him in the house, checking to make sure we are still sitting on the front porch. *"Willie, lock my damn door if you leave. It's getting dark outside, and you know these niggas robbing like crazy around here."* Ms. Joe-Ann slurs from her bedroom.

"So did the police question you on who did the shooting?" PeeWee asks. I couldn't tell if he was asking to know or asking to see if I was a rat. *"Yeah they asked, but I told them I didn't see anything, I just laid underneath a car covering my head."*

"Word, I feel you." PeeWee looks at me from the side eye and waits for the truth. I wasn't about to tell him that Travis's brother did it. Trey was known for killing. According to Big Mac, he already had five bodies under his belt, excluding the six bystanders he had just knocked off. So I keep it at seal, and tell him that I did not know who did the shooting.

So much had been going on; I felt this was an opportunity to tell PeeWee about my Sunday at church. Maybe this upcoming Sunday he could join mama and I, but only if Mo'Nique works.

A church is the right place to be at when you are to re-visit the wrong decisions you have made. The environment is very healthy and refreshing. Some bad boys may feel embarrassed to be in the house of God, but even they wish to be there, without anyone knowing. I hope PeeWee finds a way to the church too.

I cannot ask him to join us without looking into Mo'Nique's schedule. It is not going to be pretty if he finds out about Mo'Nique and I on the day he makes up his mind to attend the Church. The people hanging out with PeeWee in Maryland would not know him as well as I do. He might appear to be a very tough guy, but deep down he is a tender, kind-hearted person.

Chapter 7- Dead End

"We look at death from the selfish side, like: That guy died. Oh, it's so sad. Why is it sad? He's away from all of this bad stuff that's here on earth. I mean, at the worst, he's just somewhere quiet, no nothing. At best, he's an angel... Or he's a spirit somewhere. What is so bad about that?"

-Tupac Shakur

"Bro, I can't lie with all the shooting and toxic behavior this summer. I felt that it was best I started going to church with mama. There is a dire need for people to connect with God, especially after the block party incident; hence, I too, went to church with mama on Sunday.

Seeing my mama drop tears of joy made me feel good. I felt loved, as if my father was still alive. Mama stared with a deep smirk on her face and said: Boy, you fix your tie just like your father did when he was alive... I never could do it well...God knows I miss that man... Life would be easier if he was still here."

Mama never really got over daddy being killed in a mistaken drive-by. And I still lose sleep at night staying up listening to mama weep.

"It so happened that I attended church on the first Sunday of the month, and I saw everyone was nicely dressed." However, my Sunday's best outfit was a plain polo shirt from Ms. Sandy's store, and an old tie from daddy's closet.

I continue, *"When I walked into the church, I can't lie bro, I didn't feel welcomed. Some of them acted like they'd seen a ghost. But mama said that's what the devil wants me to feel - unwelcomed and unwanted - so that I can be alone, and he can take my soul. As it got late into the hour, Pastor Jones stepped into the pulpit and said: Sit down Church. First off, I want to say good morning, and I am glad you all could make it. I don't wanna waste your time, and I'm not gonna have you here long, so let me get straight to the point - some of you in here have been living a lie. Lying about who you are, lying about how you were raised, and most of all, lying to yourselves. No, I'm not talking about the grown folks, I'm talking about you kids umhm."*

The church was quiet, and the Pastor was looking directly at me. I started gasping for air. It felt like the devil had just attacked me in church having his hands around my neck sponge tight. It's not that I couldn't remove his hands, it's just that the truth was cutting off my circulation.

God wanted me to sit through my truth and take in my shameful ways. While Pastor Jones was speaking, I kept thinking about the times I stole from Ms. Sandy's store, and the times I would get into meaningless fights. I could have easily been Keisha's son lil P.J, but here I am sitting up in church, ashamed of the sins I committed. God will allow you to fool mankind, but not yourself or Him.

"The last ten minutes of the church were more of a praying session, where you walk to the altar and get prayer. Mama forced me to head up to the altar; I was scared as hell because I was filled with so many sins. I thought I was going to fall dead on my way there. As soon as I got there, Pastor Jones grabbed me by the hand, patted me on the shoulders, and whispered: Welcome young man. God is pleased with you, and this is a way of acknowledging that God is real, and that He is your lord

and savior. Now, there will be stumps and broken branches in your path, but you have to continue."

Ever since that Sunday, I haven't gone a day without praying, and I have also developed a habit of reading a bible verse every now and then. I am aware of where help comes from, and acknowledge the things God has done for me.

"Bro, next Sunday, you should come to church with me" I invite PeeWee to join us. *"Naw bro, that's all you, I'm just not into clapping and stomping shit. Besides, people spend all day praising a man that they never saw, a waste of time if you ask me."* PeeWee replies, trying to make me feel foolish. I can tell PeeWee is letting his pride get the best of him. *"Besides, in a month, I'm moving to Maryland for good. I decided moving with my dad is best for me right now, mama can't teach me how to be a man."*

This is it. I could feel it. Once PeeWee went back to Maryland, our friendship would be over. We were pulling in two opposite directions. No, I wasn't saved or anything like that, but in my heart, I wanted to spend more time building a relationship with God. PeeWee wasn't really sure about what he wanted, but I am sure he wanted to get back to Maryland for the homies.

A month later…

PeeWee came to see me earlier that morning before he headed to Maryland for good. When we talked, I told him how much I loved him, and how much I was going to miss him. I even shed a tear or two. My brother was going away for good. Ms. Joe-Ann was more than happy to take him to the airport, knowing that there was going to be one less mouth she had to feed. I guess the little food stamps she was receiving weren't doing the job for her. I didn't trust Maryland, and my heart didn't sit right with PeeWee going back. It had almost been a week when Ms. Joe-Ann came beating down our front door.

"It's PeeWee, It's PeeWee." I never heard Ms. Joe-Ann call PeeWee by his nickname. *"My son is gone."* Ms. Joe-Ann said while shivering and twitching. I stood at the corner of the hall between my bedroom and the living room. I couldn't move nor speak. I didn't want to face Ms. Joe-Ann knowing she allowed PeeWee to go live with his father. *"His dad just called and said PeeWee was shot*

three times in the face, making it hard to recognize him. They say he was shot down by a rival gang member." Ms. Joe-Ann had no idea PeeWee was gang-related in Maryland.

Silent tears rolled down my cheeks while I squatted in the hall. PeeWee was gone, and I never got the chance to say goodbye. We were supposed to grow old together, go fishing out on the lake, and talk about our childhood. He was gone. He never got the chance to turn eighteen. I kept replaying our last conversation in my head. I wanted to question God, and give Him a piece of my mind, but that wasn't going to bring PeeWee back. Never question the lord is what mama would be saying right now. At this point, none of it mattered. I had lost my best friend, and there was nothing that could bring him back.

Months after PeeWee's death……

There are times I sit alone on the porch in the evening just to read PeeWee bible verses. I often catch myself smiling, because I think about all the great times we had, and that I finally got the chance to introduce him to God. It's no doubt he made it into heaven, because the sun always shines right where PeeWee used to sit, and if I squint hard enough, I can see his wings flap in the wind.

The End!

Thank you

I want to thank every reader that took the time out to read my book. I am forever grateful. I put so much time and effort into this project. I find myself dropping tears right now. There were times I wanted to give up, but God wouldn't allow me. I remember every moment and the amount of energy it took to groom this project. When I was a kid, I used to sit at the kitchen counter and write nonsense stories, and pretend Oprah would be interviewing me. In simpler words, just to get people to read my book is a blessing and means a lot to me. Again, thank you so much.

Love,

Anthony Norton

PEEWEE, I SWEAR I'M NOT LYING!

www.ingramcontent.com/pod-product-compliance
Lightning Source LLC
Chambersburg PA
CBHW022009100426
42736CB00041B/1406